DESIGNED

TO

BE

A

"10"

2 Simple Questions to Discovering Your Purpose

Leader's Guide

Designed To Be a "10": 2 Simple Questions to Discovering Your Purpose – Leader's Guide

By Robynn K. Coates

Printed in the United States of America

ISBN   9780991164912

Front Cover by Lara Shoup

FireEscape Publishing, LLC

Dedication

This book is dedicated to those who teach others how to find their purpose. May your investment in the lives of others bring you a hundredfold return as you live your design and become your own unique "10"!

Acknowledgement

Thanks to Lara Shoup for the inspiration, conversation, and the road trip that lead to the development and writing of Designed to Be a "10" and to Christina Miller for your work in editing this book.

This booklet belongs to:

_____

Today's date:

_____

"A winner is someone who recognizes his God-given talents, works his tail off to develop them into skills, and uses these skills to accomplish his goals."

Larry Bird

DESIGNED
TO
BE
A
"10"

2 Simple Questions to Discovering Your Purpose

A Word to the Leader:

Thank you for taking the time to teach the *Designed to Be a "10"* Personal Development Workshop and help others find their purpose! This is an exciting process and one I trust you will find rewarding.

This Leader's Guide will walk you through the *Designed to Be a "10"* discussion. As you prepare to lead this discussion, the following will assist you in your presentation:

- Your Script: ***You will find your script in bold italics. This is what you will read aloud to the group.***
- Your Prompts: (*Any suggestions or prompts for you to take note of during the discussion will be identified in non-bold font and in parentheses.*)

Other miscellaneous items:

- Excitement: Excitement is contagious. Your enthusiasm will rub off on your students. Keep it upbeat!
- Encourage discussion: For the best discussion possible, encourage open, considerate, and honest conversation.
- Gear your talk to your audience: *Designed to Be a "10"* was written with high-school and college students in mind, but this talk can be shared with any group that includes people who want to learn more about finding their purpose. Know your audience and gear the talk to them and their interests.
- A safe place: Make it a safe place for people to share their thoughts by valuing every individual and response.
- Have fun!

DESIGNED TO BE A "10"

(((Finding Your Purpose)))

Hello! Please open your Journal Guide to page one. (Begin by asking the following question. Then discuss the participants' answers.)

Would you exchange a $10 Bill for a $1 Bill?

Why or why not? *(Allow participants to answer and discuss.)*

Most people would not exchange a $10 bill for a $1 bill because a $1 bill does not have the value of a $10 bill. In our discussion, we are going to use the $10 bill as an analogy of your life. Just like the $10 bill, your value is a "10." In fact, you are a perfect "10"! That does not mean you are flawless or incapable of making mistakes. It does mean, however, that your value is a "10." Do you see yourself as a "10"? Would you say that people in general see themselves as valuable? (Allow participants to answer and discuss.)

Unfortunately, many people sell themselves short because they see themselves like a lot of the $10 bills we commonly see—ripped, crumpled, or dirty—causing them to believe their value is diminished. (You may want to show the participants a clean and crisp $10 bill along with a tattered and torn one.) Does a clean and crisp $10 bill have more value than a tattered and torn $10 bill? (Allow participants to answer and discuss.) Obviously, the answer is "No." The lesson of the $10 bill is this: It doesn't matter if the $10 bill is clean and crisp or tattered and torn, it is still worth $10. Its value has not changed!

While some people feel they are just not valuable enough, others choose to bury their talents (their $10 bill). Let me give you a scenario: Imagine I gave two students a $10 bill each. One buries the bill and the other spends it. At the end of 18 months, which is supposedly the life cycle of a $10 bill, it has had changed hands an average of 30 times. That's $300 worth of transactions! Who knows where that bill traveled? Maybe it went around the world while the other $10 was buried and unproductive. Which bill fulfilled its purpose? Obviously, the one that was used fulfilled its purpose. And likewise, we all get to choose whether we will fulfill the purpose we were created for or allow our talents and gifts to go unused.

It's now time for us to answer three important questions...

DESIGNED TO BE A "10"

(((Finding Your Purpose)))

I will give you a few moments to answer the following questions, and then we will discuss our answers. (Give participants about 30 seconds to answer the following three questions and then ask each question one at a time. Allow participants to share their answers and thoughts, then read the answer that follows each question.)

Questions to Ask Myself

1.) Do I believe a person can do anything they set their mind to?   YES   NO

The answer is "No." There are some things you can't do, especially when you are operating outside your gifts and talents. A 5'4" female with average to below-average jumping ability will never be able to slam dunk a basketball. This skill is not within her repertoire of gifts and talents. Acknowledging that there are things you can't do is not negative or depressing, but rather liberating as it frees you to focus on doing what you are good at and forgetting about the rest.

2.) Do I believe that a person can be good at anything if they are willing to work hard enough at it?   YES   NO

(The answer is the same as #1.)

3.) Do I believe I can have whatever I want?
        YES   NO

You cannot have whatever you want because there are certain things you don't have control over. This includes other people, weather, circumstances, and laws of the universe such as the law of gravity. You do, however, have control over your responses and choices. Focus your attention on what you can control, not on what you can't.

(Read the following quote to the group.)

"Everybody is a genius. But if you judge a fish by its ability to climb a tree, it will live its whole life believing that it is stupid."
Albert Einstein

What are your thoughts on this quote? *(Allow participants to answer and discuss.)* **Many times people feel inadequate because they compare themselves to others. If you do this, you will always find someone who is prettier, smarter, more athletic, more musical, more popular, or more gifted than you, and you will feel inadequate. The story here is simple: Swim in your own pond and don't be a fish trying to climb a tree!**

DESIGNED TO BE A "10"

(((Finding Your Purpose)))

(Read the column on the left to the group. Then give the participants the answers to the blanks in the right column.)

The "Past's" Purpose

The past will be either a classroom or a prison cell. You get to choose.

Does a tattered and torn $10 bill have less value than a crisp, clean one?

Regardless of your past, your value is a "10." You get to choose whether you will be a victim or a victor, to live with your potential untapped or expressed.

Learning from your mistakes and your past will result in wisdom and can help set you up for future success.

- You were ____created____ for a ____purpose____.

- Fulfilling your purpose will bring ____satisfaction____.

- Part of finding out what your purpose is will be finding what your purpose ____is____ ____not____.

- How do you do this? By ____trial____ and ____error____.

- Do not look at failure as ____final____. Rather you can ____fail____ ____forward____, meaning you can use your failure as a stepping stone to get you closer to your dream. Remember Thomas Edison? How many times did he "fail" before he had a success? Or consider Abraham Lincoln...

(Read the following question and have participants look over Abraham Lincoln's resume.)

Have you ever seen Abraham Lincoln's resume? It is riddled with failure. Take a look:

<u>Abraham Lincoln's Resume</u>

- 1831 – Lost his job
- 1832 – Defeated in run for Illinois State Legislature
- 1833 – Failed in business
- 1835 – Sweetheart died
- 1836 – Had nervous breakdown
- 1838 – Defeated in run for Illinois House Speaker
- 1843 – Defeated in run for nomination for US Congress
- 1848 – Lost re-nomination
- 1849 – Rejected for land officer position
- 1854 – Defeated in run for US Senate
- 1856 – Defeated in run for nomination for Vice President
- 1858 – Again defeated in run for US Senate

(Taken from www.school-for-champions.com)

Yet, would you call him a failure? Of course not. In fact, he is probably one of the most important presidents in our country's history.

When it comes to his resume, we don't look at all the failures, but the successes that followed those failures.

DESIGNED TO BE A "10"

(((Finding Your Purpose)))

(Give the participants the answers to the blanks in the right column.)

Redefining "10"

- "10" does not mean you are _____ perfect _____.

- "10" does imply, however, that you fulfill your _____ purpose _____ and become the person you were _____ created _____ to be.

- "10" for one _____ person _____ is not necessarily a "10" for _____ another _____ _____ person _____.

- Therefore, _____ comparisons _____ are _____ useless _____!

"HE IS A WISE MAN

who wastes no energy on pursuits

FOR WHICH HE IS NOT FITTED;

and he is wiser still

who from among the things he can do well,

chooses and resolutely follows the BEST."

William Gladstone

This quote instructs us to focus on those areas in which we have gifts and talents, rather than focusing on strengthening our areas of weakness. What are your thoughts on this quote? *(When speaking of weaknesses, we are not referring to character weaknesses such as dishonesty, disloyalty, lack of self-control, etc. We do need to work on character weaknesses. However, the focus of Designed to Be a "10" is on gifts and talents, and this is what we are referring to.)*

DESIGNED TO BE A "10"
(((Finding Your Purpose)))

(Read the column on the left out loud to the group. Then give the participants the answers to the blanks in the right column. Do the same for the next page.)

Mining Diamonds

Finding your purpose is similar to mining diamonds. Diamonds are not found on the surface. They have to be mined. Once a diamond is found, it goes through a long process of cutting and polishing. This can take months! Finding your purpose may take you years, but don't give up! A diamond that has gone through this process is beautiful and brilliant.

- ___X___ marks the ___spot___.

- The "______" portion of the "___X___" is the line representing your ___talent___.

- The "___/___" portion of the "___X___" is the line representing your ___passion___.

- Where the two ___lines___ intersect is your "___bull's___ - ___eye___."

- This is where your greatest ___fulfillment___ comes. It is where you get the greatest ___return___ on your ___investment___. It is where you get the "B__iggest__ B__ang__ F__or__ Y__our__ B__uck__".

8

- Your __bull's__ - __eye__ is where your __talent__ and your __passion__ converge.

- The most you can improve in an area is a __2__ or maybe a __3__ on a scale of 1-10. (John Maxwell, *Put Your Dream To The Test*)

- It only makes __sense__, then, to spend your __time__ in and __concentrate__ on those areas where you have the higher __number__ to start with.

- You have the potential to be a "__10__" in some area.

- Find your "__10__"!

DESIGNED TO BE A "10"

(((Finding Your Purpose)))

On this page and the next you will answer the following questions. Write down the first thing that comes to mind, regardless how audacious it may seem! Dream your dreams! (Give participants a few minutes to answer the following questions.)

Today's Date

_____

"A gift opens the way and ushers the giver into the presence of the great."

Proverbs 18:16 (NIV)

1.) What is my #1 **PASSION** - the thing I love to do more than anything else?

2.) What is my **HEART'S DESIRE**?

3.) What am I **NATURALLY GIFTED** at? (What comes natural to me, but not necessarily for others?)

4.) What do **OTHER PEOPLE** tell me I'm good at?

5.) What **FUELS, INVIGORATES, and ENERGIZES** me versus saps and drains me?

"There are two kinds of talent: man-made talent and God-given talent. With man-made talent, you have to work very hard. With God-given talent, you just TOUCH IT UP once in a while."

Pearl Bailey

6.) Where do I have **GOOD RESULTS and FAVOR**? Things just seem to click and people seem to want to help me.

7.) If I could choose to do one thing in which I was **GUARANTEED SUCCESS**, what would it be?

8.) What do I love to do so much that I would gladly do it for the **REST OF MY LIFE,** and I would do it for **FREE**?

9.) Where do I have **PEACE**? (A knowing that I am doing the **RIGHT** thing for me.)

Taken in part from **Fulfilling Your God-Given Destiny** *by Casey Treat*

DESIGNED TO BE A "10"

(((Finding Your Purpose)))

(Read the column on the left to the group. Then have participants answer the questions in the right column. Do the same for the next page.)

Any good scientist is an expert at collecting data.

1.) What can I do **IMMEDIATELY** either to discover my purpose or pursue my purpose?

A._____

B._____

C._____

D._____

E._____

F._____

Be an expert "data collector" in your own life by taking note of what works and what doesn't work.

2.) Three **ADULTS** who know me well enough that I can ask what strengths they see in me:

A._____

B._____

C._____

Tracking your progress, setbacks, successes, and failures will help you save precious time.

3.) Three of my **FRIENDS** whom I trust to give me honest feedback about what they think my strengths are:

A._____

B._____

C._____

It will give you the ADVANTAGE OF PERSPECTIVE – the ability to see all sides of an issue.

4.) What are my **RESOURCES**? (i.e. "My aunt is a life coach. I'll ask her for help." "I think I want to be a curator at a museum, so I'll talk to the Safari Museum curators and see if I can shadow them." "Mr. Babcock, my math teacher, seems passionate about what he does, so I'll ask him if he would mind sharing how he found his passion." Consider websites, magazines, people, classes, opportunities, events.)

A._____

B._____

C._____

D._____

E._____

F._____

G._____

H._____

I._____

J._____

K._____

L._____

(Read the following.)

All these questions lead us to two of the simplest and most important questions we need to answer in order to determine our purpose:

1.) What are my talents and gifts?
2.) What are my passions and heart's desires?

Once you answer these questions, you are on your way to discovering your purpose.

DESIGNED TO BE A "10"

(((Finding Your Purpose)))

My Talents/Gifts   My Passions/Heart's Desires

(Read the following instructions to your participants.)

1. **On this page, you will list your talents (also known as gifts) and your passions (also known as your heart's desires) under the appropriate column.**
2. **Once you have listed your talents and passions, evaluate and assign each one a number, 1-10 (10 being the highest), according to the level of each talent and passion.**
3. **You are almost ready to plot your talents and passions on a chart, but before you do, refer to the example on the following page. On the "\" line of the "X", you will place your talents/gifts, and on the "/" line of the "X" you will place your passions/heart's desires. The intersection of the "X" (where the two lines meet) is where your "10" is located. As you move away from the center of the "X," the number decreases. The circle is where "7" is located. So, for example, if you were to chart a talent of public speaking with an eight, you would place it on the talent "\" line close to the intersection. If public speaking is also a passion and you assign it a nine you would notice the two are close to the intersection. If however, your talent is a nine (such as science), but your passion for science is a four, the disparity suggests this is not your purpose and not something you should pursue. At least, maybe not for now.**
4. **After you have charted your talents and passions, you'll see in what areas both your talents and passions converge closest to the intersection of the "X." Take note of those areas that fall within the circle (both talent and passion are at least a "7"). These are the areas worth investigating because they could be the direction of your purpose. Now turn to the page after the example and chart your talents and passions.**

DESIGNED TO BE A "10"

(((Finding Your Purpose)))

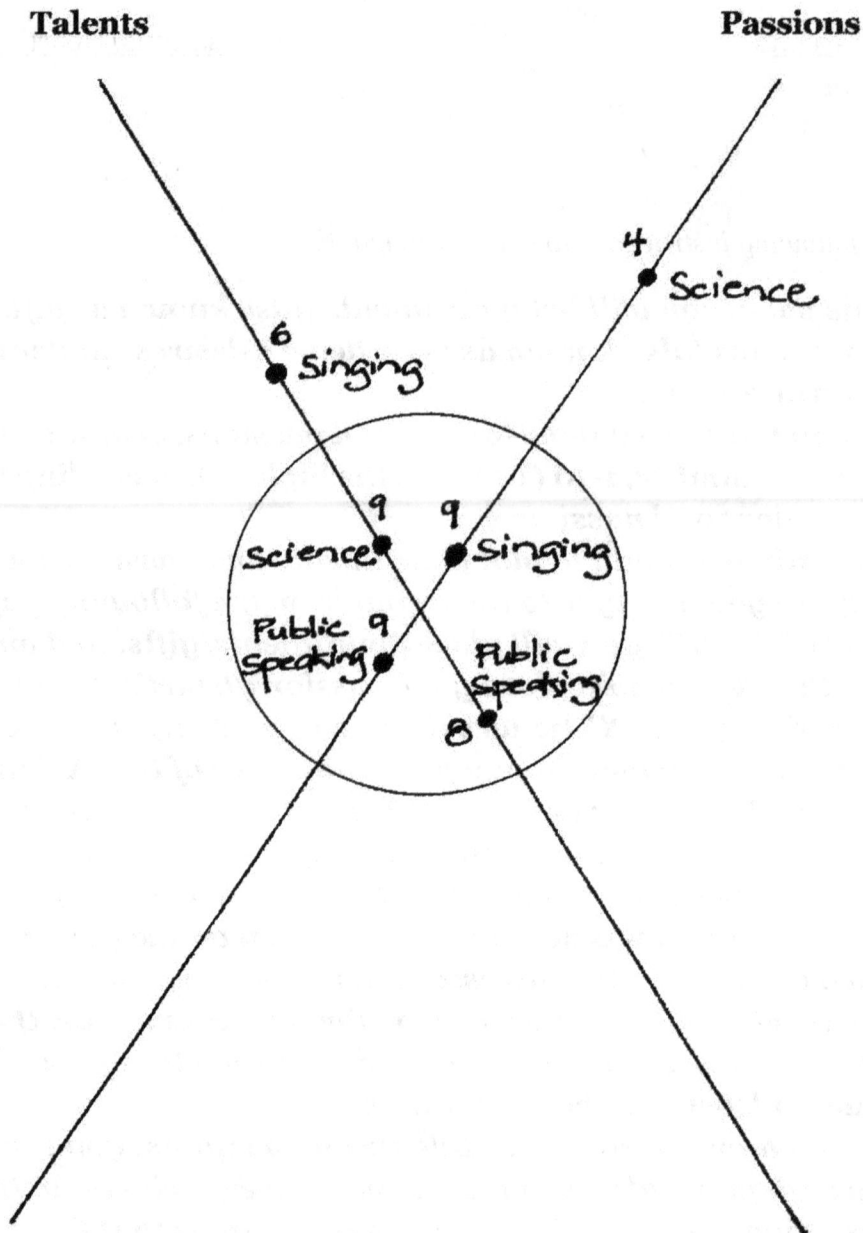

Talents   Passions

4
Science

6
Singing

9   9
Science   Singing

Public 9
Speaking   Public
Speaking

8

DESIGNED TO BE A "10"

(((Finding Your Purpose)))

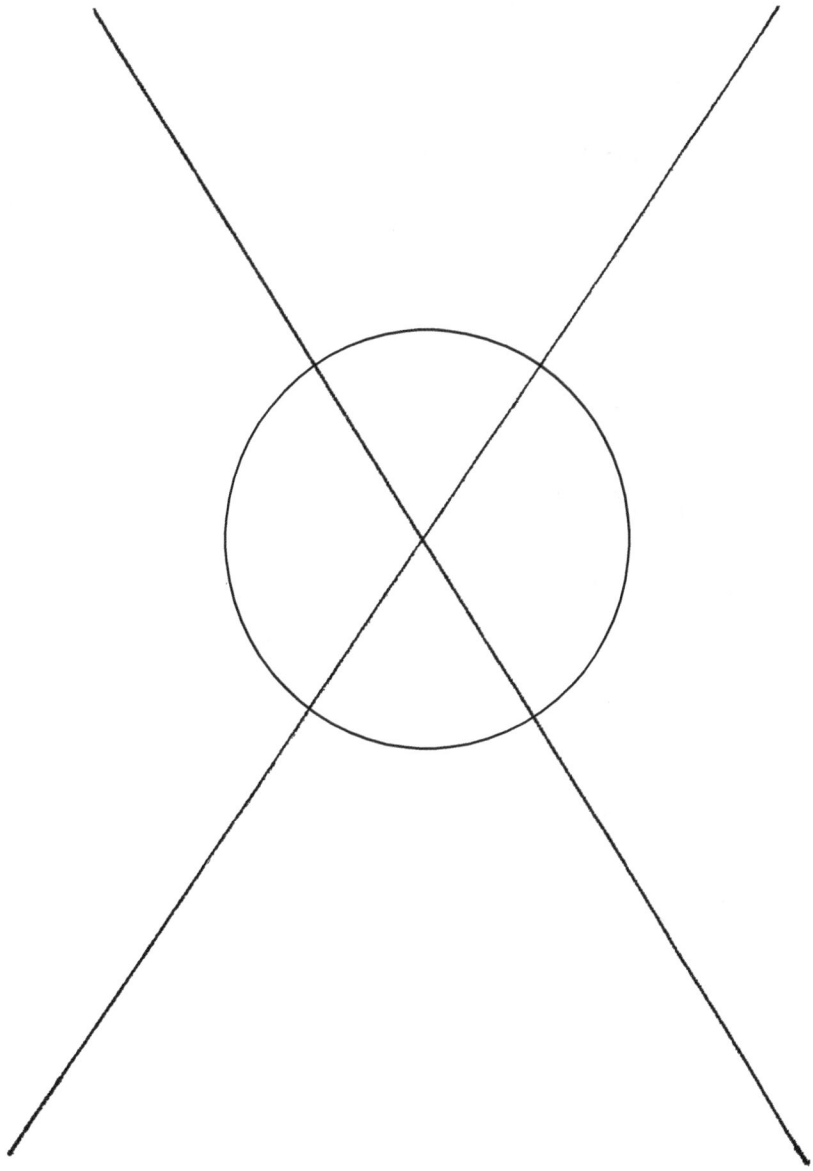

Talents

Passions

Words from a very wise man:

Wisdom is SUPREME;

   therefore get wisdom.

Though it cost all you have get understanding.

It is not good to have ZEAL without KNOWLEDGE,

   nor to be hasty and miss the way.

For by wise counsel you can wage your war, and in an abundance of **counselors** there is victory and safety.

King Solomon

DESIGNED TO BE A "10"

(((Finding Your Purpose)))

(Read the following, then answer in the blanks below.)

**JOURNEY
TO
YOUR
DESTINATION**

If you were taking a trip to a destination you had never been to before, you would need directions to get there. You may look at a map or find someone who had already been there and ask for guidance. Life is a journey. You can aimlessly wonder around and waste a lot of precious time, or you can maximize your time and ask for directions. Here are some tips to help you get to your destination as quickly as possible.

- Get lots of ____advice____ / ____input____ from wise people who have already been where you want to go.

- There will always be portions of the journey you are not particularly fond of. Don't be afraid to do some things you don't love to do. They are not ____permanent____, just ____temporary____ steps to help get you to your destination.

- Keep moving ahead. Waiting for the perfect time, opportunity, or circumstance is a time killer. Get moving! "It is much easier to ____steer____ a ____moving____ car than a ____parked____ car."

What one habit, if you had it, would make the biggest positive change in your life?

That is your mission! Make it your goal.

Today's Date: _____

habit

_____
_____
_____
_____
_____

steps

_____
_____
_____
_____

obstacles to overcome

_____
_____
_____
_____
_____

"Watch your thoughts, for they become words. Watch your words, for they become actions. Watch your actions, for they become habits. Watch your habits, for they become character. Watch your character, for it becomes your destiny."

Unknown author

Where to from here?

Seeing your dreams finally come true may take lots of hard work and many years, but don't get hung up on the end result—the achievement of your dreams. The joy really is in the journey, and the most important thing is that you are on your way to making your dreams come true. That is something you can begin to do today.

What is the next thing you can do TODAY to pursue your dream?

My Next Step in Pursuing My Dreams Is:

_____

Don't wait! Regardless how small or how big that step may seem, take it and then another and then another. You will begin seeing progress as well as creating forward momentum. Many times, the hardest step is the first one!

Your dreams are precious. Don't let anyone tell you they are too big, too unrealistic, and too audacious. Hold onto your dream at all cost!

Your dreams are also dynamic. At some times they will seem clearer and more defined than at other times. They may change into something different than they were in the beginning. That's okay. Just keep heading in the direction of your dreams. Many times these changes in our original plans become an even greater blessing and a greater dream than what they started off as. So keep an open heart and an open mind.

Because your dreams, hopes, and aspirations are dynamic, it is therefore important to keep a journal of them. This will help you clarify what you want at different times of your life and see where your dreams are headed.

On the following pages, you will find worksheets similar to the ones you just filled out in this guide. These worksheets will assist you to keep track of your dreams, passions, and talents. You may not have discovered some of these yet, so keeping a journal will be beneficial as you look back and see where you've come from and look forward to where you are going. I recommend that you do this at least every five years.

I wish you all the best as you pursue your dreams and fulfill your purpose of being your own unique, perfect "10"!

Robynn K. Coates

The following worksheets are the same as those previously presented. They may be reproduced for your periodic use on your journey to your dream.

DESIGNED TO BE A "10"

(((Finding Your Purpose)))

Today's Date

_____

"A gift opens the way and ushers the giver into the presence of the great."

Proverbs 18:16 (NIV)

1.) What is my #1 **PASSION** - the thing I love to do more than anything else?

2.) What is my **HEART'S DESIRE?**

3.) What am I **NATURALLY GIFTED** at? (What comes natural to me, but not necessarily for others?)

4.) What do **OTHER PEOPLE** tell me I'm good at?

5.) What **FUELS, INVIGORATES, and ENERGIZES** me versus saps and drains me?

> **"There are two kinds of talent: man-made talent and God-given talent. With man-made talent, you have to work very hard. With God-given talent, you just TOUCH IT UP once in a while."**
>
> *Pearl Bailey*

6.) Where do I have **GOOD RESULTS and FAVOR**? Things just seem to click and people seem to want to help me.

7.) If I could choose to do one thing in which I was **GUARANTEED SUCCESS**, what would it be?

8.) What do I love to do so much that I would gladly do it for the **REST OF MY LIFE,** and I would do it for **FREE**?

9.) Where do I have **PEACE**? (A knowing that I am doing the **RIGHT** thing for me.)

*Taken in part from Fulfilling Your God-Given Destiny *by Casey Treat*

DESIGNED TO BE A "10"

(((Finding Your Purpose)))

Any good scientist is an expert at collecting data.

Be an expert "data collector" in your own life by taking note of what works and what doesn't work.

Tracking your progress, setbacks, successes, and failures will help you save precious time.

It will give you the <u>ADVANTAGE OF PERSPECTIVE</u> – the ability to see all sides of an issue.

1.) What can I do **IMMEDIATELY** either to discover my purpose or pursue my purpose?

A._____
B._____
C._____
D._____
E._____
F._____

2.) Three **ADULTS** who know me well enough that I can ask what strengths they see in me:

A._____
B._____
C._____

3.) Three of my **FRIENDS** whom I trust to give me honest feedback about what they think my strengths are:

A._____
B._____
C._____

4.) What are my **RESOURCES**? (i.e. "My aunt is a life coach. I'll ask her for help." "I think I want to be a curator at a museum, so I'll talk to the Safari Museum curators and see if I can shadow them." "Mr. Babcock, my math teacher, seems passionate about what he does, so I'll ask him if he would mind sharing how he found his passion." Consider websites, magazines, people, classes, opportunities, events.)

A._____

B._____

C._____

D._____

E._____

F._____

G._____

H._____

I._____

J._____

K._____

L._____

DESIGNED TO BE A "10"

(((Finding Your Purpose)))

My Talents/Gifts   My Passions/Heart's Desires

DESIGNED TO BE A "10"

(((Finding Your Purpose)))

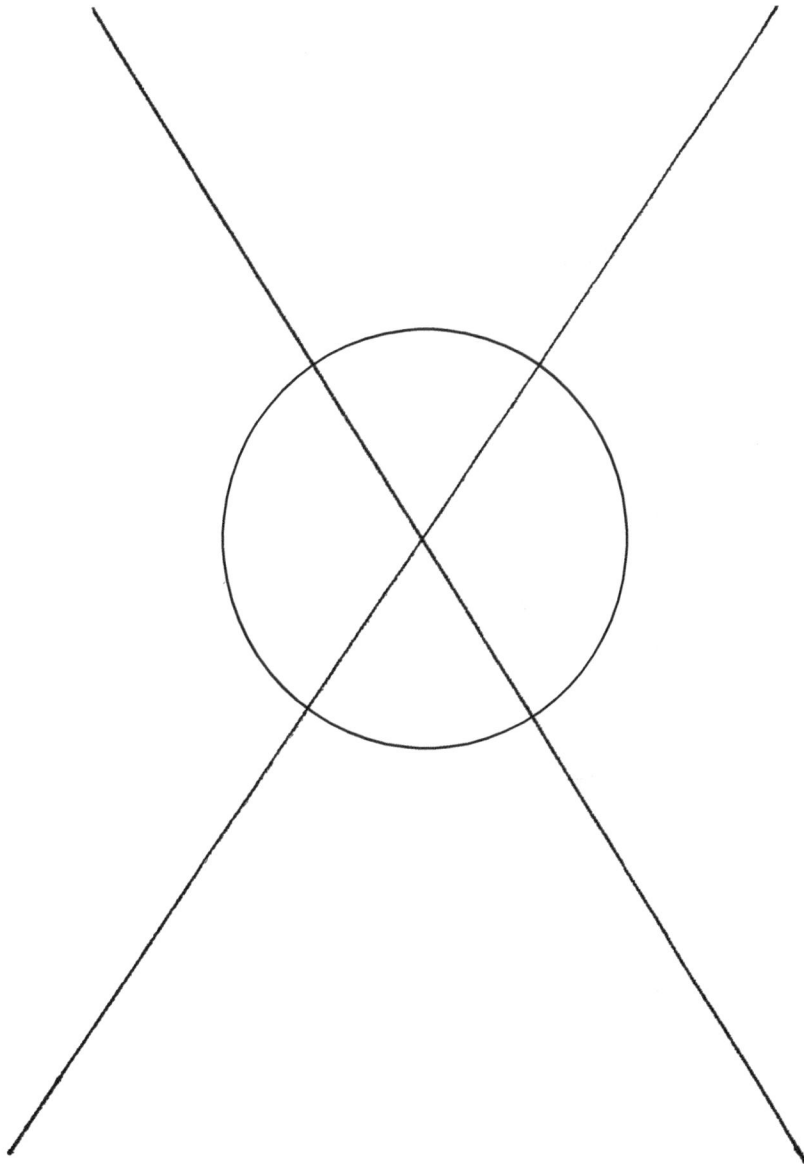

Talents   Passions

What one habit, if you had it, would make the biggest positive change in your life?

That is your mission! Make it your goal.

Today's Date: _____

habit

_____
_____
_____
_____
_____
_____

steps

_____
_____
_____
_____
_____

obstacles to overcome

_____
_____
_____
_____
_____
_____

My Notes

My Notes

My Notes

My Notes

My Notes

My Notes

ENDNOTES

❧

Kurtis, Ron. "Failures of Abraham Lincoln (1800s)." *Ron Kurtis' School For Champions*. N.p., 11 Oct. 2011. Web. 09 Sept. 2013.

Maxwell, John C. "Building On Your Strengths Gives You The Highest Return." *Put Your Dream to the Test: 10 Questions That Will Help You See It and Seize It*. Nashville, TN: Thomas Nelson, 2009. 61. Print.

Treat, Casey. "How to Discover Your Destiny." *Fulfilling Your God given Destiny*. Nashville, TN: Thomas Nelson, 1995. 25-39. Print.

www.ingramcontent.com/pod-product-compliance
Lightning Source LLC
Chambersburg PA
CBHW080533030426
42337CB00023B/4714